DAVID:
DEVELOPING PERSONAL CHARACTER

A four-week course on the life and
inner character of David.

by
Susan L. Lingo

Apply·It·To·Life™

Adult

BIBLE CURRICULUM
from **Group**

Group
Loveland, Colorado

Apply·It·To·Life™

Adult

BIBLE CURRICULUM

Group

David: Developing Personal Character
Copyright © 1996 Group Publishing, Inc.

Credits
Editor: Bob Buller
Senior Editor: Paul Woods
Chief Creative Officer: Joani Schultz
Copy Editor: Helen Turnbull
Art Director: Helen Lannis
Cover Designer: Liz Howe
Computer Graphic Artist: Randy Kady
Cover Photographer: Larry Prosor, SuperStock
Illustrators: Rex Bohn and Ray Tollison

ISBN 1-55945-506-3
10 9 8 7 6 5 4 3 2 1   05 04 03 02 01 00 99 98 97 96
Printed in the United States of America.

C O N T E N T S

Introduction

WHAT IS APPLY-IT-TO-LIFE™ ADULT BIBLE CURRICULUM?

Apply-It-To-Life™ Adult Bible Curriculum is a series of four-week study courses designed to help you facilitate powerful lessons that will help class members grow in faith. Use this course with

- Sunday school classes,
- home study groups,
- weekday Bible study groups,
- men's Bible studies,
- women's Bible studies, and
- family classes.

The variety of courses gives the adult student a broad coverage of topical, life-related issues and significant biblical topics. In addition, as the name of the series implies, every lesson helps the adult student apply Scripture to his or her life.

Each course in Apply-It-To-Life Adult Bible Curriculum provides four lessons on different aspects of one topic. In each course, you also receive Fellowship and Outreach Specials connected to the month's topic. They provide outreach activities, suggestions for building closer relationships in your class, and even a party idea!

WHAT MAKES APPLY-IT-TO-LIFE™ ADULT BIBLE CURRICULUM UNIQUE?

Teaching as Jesus Taught

Jesus was a master teacher. With Apply-It-To-Life Adult Bible Curriculum, you'll use the same teaching methods and principles that Jesus used:

- **Active Learning.** Think back on an important lesson you've learned in life. Did you learn it from reading about it? from hearing about it? from something you did? Chances are, the most important lessons you've learned came from things you experienced. That's what active learning is—learning by doing. Active learning leads students through activities and experiences that help them understand important principles, messages, and ideas. It's a discovery process that helps people internalize and remember what they learn.

Jesus often used active learning. One of the most vivid examples is his washing of his disciples' feet. In Apply-It-To-Life Adult Bible Curriculum, the teacher might remove his or her shoes and socks, then read aloud the foot-washing passage from John 13, or the teacher might choose to actually wash people's feet. Participants won't soon forget it. Active learning uses simple activities to teach profound lessons.

● **Interactive Learning.** Interactive learning means learning through small-group interaction and discussion. Each person is actively involved in discovering God's truth. Interactive learning puts people in pairs, trios, or foursomes to involve everyone in the learning experience. It takes active learning a step further by having people who have gone through an experience teach others what they've learned.

Jesus often helped cement the learning from an experience by questioning people—sometimes in small groups—about what had happened. He regularly questioned his followers and his opponents, forcing them to think and to discuss among themselves what he was teaching them. After washing his disciples' feet, the first thing Jesus did was ask the disciples if they understood what he had done. After the foot-washing activity, the teacher might form small groups and have people discuss how they felt when the leader removed his or her shoes and socks. Then group members might compare those feelings and the learning involved to what the disciples must have experienced.

● **Biblical Depth.** Apply-It-To-Life Adult Bible Curriculum recognizes that most people are ready to go below the surface to better understand the deeper truths of the Bible. Therefore, the activities and studies go beyond an "easy answer" approach to Christian education and lead people to grapple with difficult issues from a biblical perspective.

In the Bible Basis, you'll find information that will help you understand the Scriptures you're dealing with. Within the class-time section of the lesson, thought-provoking activities and discussions lead adults to new depths of biblical understanding. "Bible Insights" within the lesson give pertinent information that will bring the Bible to life for you and your class members. In-class handouts give adults significant Bible information and challenge them to search for and discover biblical truths for themselves. Finally, the "For Even Deeper Discussion" sections provide questions that will lead your class members to new and deeper levels of insight and application.

No one questions the depth of Jesus' teachings or the effectiveness of his teaching methods. This curriculum follows Jesus' example and helps people probe the depths of the Bible in a way no other adult curriculum does.

● **Bible Application.** Jesus didn't stop with helping people understand truth. It wasn't enough that the rich young ruler knew all the right answers. Jesus wanted him to take action on what he knew. In the same way, Apply-It-To-Life Adult Bible Curriculum encourages a response in people's lives. That's why this curriculum is called "Apply-It-To-Life"! Depth of understanding means little if the truths of Scripture don't zing into people's hearts. Each lesson brings home one point and encourages people to consider the changes they might make in response.

● **One Purpose.** In each study, every activity works toward communicating and applying the same point. People may discover other new truths, but the study doesn't load them down with a mass of information. Sometimes less is more. When lessons try to teach too much, they often fail to teach anything. Even Jesus limited his teaching to what he felt people could really learn and apply (John 16:12). Apply-It-To-Life Adult Bible Curriculum makes sure that class members thoroughly understand and apply one point each week.

● **Variety.** Jesus constantly varied his teaching methods. One day he would have a serious discussion with his disciples about who he was, and another day he'd baffle them by turning water into wine. What he didn't do was allow them to become bored with what he had to teach them.

Any kind of study can become less than exciting if the leader and students do everything the same way week after week. Apply-It-To-Life Adult Bible Curriculum varies activities and approaches to keep everyone's interest level high each week. In one class, you might have people in small groups "put themselves in the disciples' sandals" and experience something of the confusion of Jesus' death and resurrection. In another lesson, class members may experience problems in communication and examine how such problems can damage relationships.

● **Relevance.** People today want to know how to live successfully right now. They struggle with living as authentic Christians at work, in the family, and in the community. They want to know how the Bible can help them live faithful lives—how it can help them face the difficulties of living in today's culture. Apply-It-To-Life Adult Bible Curriculum bridges the gap between biblical truth and the "real world" issues of people's lives. Jesus didn't discuss with his followers the eschatological significance of Ezekiel's wheels, and Apply-It-To-Life Adult Bible Curriculum won't either! Courses and studies in this curriculum focus on the real needs of people and help them discover answers in Scripture that will help meet those needs.

● **A Nonthreatening Atmosphere.** In many adult classes, people feel intimidated because they're new Christians or because they don't have the Bible knowledge they think they should have. Jesus sometimes intimidated those who opposed him, but he consistently treated his followers with understanding and respect. We want people in church to experience the same understanding and respect Jesus' followers experienced. With Apply-It-To-Life Adult Bible Curriculum, no one is embarrassed for not knowing or understanding as much as someone else. In fact, the interactive learning process minimizes the differences between those with vast Bible knowledge and those with little Bible knowledge. Lessons often begin with nonthreatening, sharing questions and move slowly toward more depth. Whatever their level of knowledge or commitment, class members will work together to discover biblical truths that can affect their lives.

● **A Group That Cares.** Jesus chose 12 people who learned from him together. That group practically lived together—sharing one another's hurts, joys, and ambitions. Sometimes Jesus divided the 12 into smaller groups and worked with just three or four at a time.

Adults today long for a close-knit group with whom they can share personal needs and joys. Activities in this curriculum will help class members get to know one another better and care for one another more as they study the Bible and apply its truths to their lives. As people reveal their thoughts and feelings to one another, they'll grow closer and develop more commitment to the group. And they'll be encouraging one another along the way!

● **An Element of Delight.** We don't often think about Jesus' ministry in this way, but he often brought fun and delight to his followers. Remember the time he raised Peter's mother-in-law or the time he sat happily with children on his lap? How about the joy and excitement at his triumphal entry into Jerusalem or the time he helped his disciples catch a boatload of fish—after they'd fished all night with no success?

People learn more when they're having fun. So within Apply-It-To-Life Adult Bible Curriculum, elements of fun and delight pop up often. And sometimes adding fun is as simple as using a carrot for a pretend microphone!

Taking the Fear out of Teaching

Teachers love Apply-It-To-Life Adult Bible Curriculum because it makes teaching much less stressful. Lessons in this curriculum...

● **are easy to teach.** Interactive learning frees the teacher from being a dispenser of information to serve as a facilitator of learning. Teachers can spend class time guiding people to discover and apply biblical truths. The studies provide clear, understandable Bible background; easy-to-prepare learning experiences; and thought-provoking discussion questions.

● **can be prepared quickly.** Lessons in Apply-It-To-Life Adult Bible Curriculum are logical and clear. There's no sorting through tons of information to figure out the lesson. In 30 minutes, a busy teacher can easily read a lesson and prepare to teach it. In addition, optional and For Extra Time activities allow the teacher to tailor the lesson to the class. And the thorough instructions and questions will guide even an inexperienced teacher through each powerful lesson.

● **let everyone share in the class' success.** With Apply-It-To-Life Adult Bible Curriculum, the teacher is one of the participants. The teacher still guides the class, but the burden is not as heavy. Everyone participates and adds to the study's effectiveness. So when the study has an impact, everyone shares in that success.

● **lead the teacher to new discoveries.** Each lesson is designed to help the teacher first discover a biblical truth. And most teachers will make additional discoveries as they prepare each lesson. In class, the teacher will discover even more as other adults share what they have found. As with any type of teaching, the teacher will likely learn more than anyone else in the class!

● **provide relevant information to class members.** Photocopiable handouts are designed to help people better understand or interpret Bible passages. And the handouts make teaching easier because the teacher can often refer to them for small-group discussion questions and instructions.

First familiarize yourself with an Apply-It-To-Life Adult Bible Curriculum lesson. The following explanations will help you understand how the lesson elements work together.

Lesson Elements

● The **Opening** maps out the lesson's agenda and introduces the topic for the session. Sometimes this activity will help people get better acquainted as they begin to explore the topic together.

● The **Bible Exploration and Application** activities will help people discover what the Bible says about the topic and how the lesson's point applies to their lives. In these varied activities, class members find answers to the "So what?" question. They discover the relevance of the Scriptures and commit to growing closer to God.

You may use one or both of the options in this section. They are designed to stand alone or to work together. Both present the same point in different ways. "For Even Deeper Discussion" questions appear at the end of each activity in this section. Use these questions whenever you feel they might be particularly helpful for your class.

● The **Closing** pulls everything in the lesson together and often funnels the lesson's message into a time of reflection and prayer.

● The **For Extra Time** section is just that. Use it when you've completed the lesson and still have time left or when you've used one Bible Exploration and Application option and don't have time to do the other. Or you might plan to use it instead of another option.

When you put all the sections together, you get a lesson that's fun and easy to teach. Plus, participants will learn truths they'll remember and apply to their daily lives.

Guidelines for a Successful Adult Class

● **Be a facilitator, not a lecturer.** Your job is to direct the activities and facilitate the discussions. You become a choreographer of sorts: someone who gets everyone else involved in the discussion and keeps the discussion on track.

● **Teach adults how to form small groups.** Help adults form groups of four, three, or two—whatever the activity calls for. Small-group sharing allows for more discussion and involvement by all participants. It's not as threatening or scary to open up to two people as it would be to 20 or 200!

Some leaders decide not to form small groups because they want to hear everybody's ideas. The intention is good, but some people just won't talk in a large group. Use a "report back" time after small-group discussions to gather the best responses from all groups.

Try creative group-forming methods to help everyone in the class get to know one another. For example, have class members form groups with others who are wearing the same color, shop at the same grocery store, were born the same month, or like the same season of the year.

● **Encourage relationship building.** George Barna, in his insightful book about the church, *The Frog in the Kettle,* explains that adults today have a strong need to develop friendships. In a society of high-tech toys, "personal" computers, and lonely commutes, people long for positive human contact. That's where our church classes and groups can jump in. Help adults form friendships through your class. What's discovered in a classroom setting will be better applied when friends support each other outside the classroom. In fact, the relationships begun in your class may be as important as the truths you help your adults learn.

● **Expect the unexpected.** Active learning is an adventure that doesn't always take you where you think you're going. Be open to the different directions the Holy Spirit may lead your class. When something goes wrong or an unexpected emotion is aroused, take advantage of this teachable moment. Ask probing questions; follow up on someone's deep need.

What should you do if people go off on a tangent? Don't panic. People learn best when they're engaged in meaningful discussion. And if you get through even one activity, your class will discover the point for the whole lesson. So relax. It's OK if you don't get everything done.

● **Participate—and encourage participation.** Apply-It-To-Life Adult Bible Curriculum is only as interactive as you and your class make it. Jump into discussions yourself, but don't "take over." Encourage everyone to participate. Use "active listening" responses such as rephrasing and summing up what's been said. To get more out of your discussions, use follow-up inquiries such as "Can you tell me more?" "What do you mean by that?" or "What makes you feel that way?" The more people participate, the more they'll discover God's truths for themselves.

● **Trust the Holy Spirit.** All the previous guidelines and the instructions in the lessons will be irrelevant if you ignore the presence of God in your classroom. God sent the Holy Spirit as our helper. As you use this curriculum, ask the Holy Spirit to help you facilitate the lessons. And ask the Holy Spirit to direct your class toward God's truth. Trust that God's Spirit can work through each person's discoveries, not just the teacher's.

How to Use This Course

Before the Four-Week Session
● Read the Course Introduction and This Course at a Glance (pp. 11-12).
● Decide how you'll use the art on the Publicity Page (p. 13) to publicize the course. Prepare fliers, newsletter articles, and posters as needed.
● Look at the Fellowship and Outreach Specials (pp. 69-70) and decide which ones you'll use.

Before Each Lesson

● Read the one-sentence Point, the Objectives, and the Bible Basis for the lesson. The Bible Basis provides background information on the lesson's passages and shows how those passages relate to people today.

● Choose which activities you'll use from the lesson. Remember—it's not necessary to do every activity. Pick the ones that best fit your group and your time allotment.

● Gather necessary supplies and make photocopies of any handouts you intend to use. They're listed in This Lesson at a Glance.

● Read each section of the lesson. Adjust activities as necessary to fit your class size and meeting room, but be careful not to delete all the activity. People learn best when they're actively involved.

● Make one photocopy of the "Apply-It-To-Life This Week!" handout for each class member.

COURSE INTRODUCTION—DAVID: DEVELOPING PERSONAL CHARACTER

When people hear David's name, they generally think of David's heroic deeds instead of his human identity. This isn't surprising, for the list of David's heroic feats reads like a superhero's bio. David wrestled bears and lions that threatened his father's flock. Then, armed with a simple sling and Herculean faith, he toppled a 9-foot-tall Philistine gargantuan. Later he wiped out an entire Philistine army in Keilah and delivered God's people in a blaze of glory. In his spare time, David composed passionate pleas and praises to God in psalms that have moved millions of hearts.

Superhero? So it might seem. But David was also fully human—in many ways just like the people we see in stores or meet on the street. As a human like the rest of us, David learned many painful lessons about himself and his relationship with God. For example, David struggled with evil urges and, had it not been for Abigail, might have succumbed to a desire for revenge. Also, after his adulterous affair with Bathsheba and the murder of her husband, Uriah, David admitted his sins and accepted the painful consequences of his actions. Even when David's baby died as punishment for his sin, David learned to accept God's will and to go on with his life.

In spite of David's humanity and his tendency to learn lessons the hard way, God used him in powerful ways that make David a worthy role model for us today. In the final analysis, David's inner character made him a human with whom we can identify and from whom we can learn a great deal about God and ourselves.

The lessons in this course focus on David's inner qualities and teach people how to develop those qualities in their lives. By helping people see past David's heroic image to his human identity, these lessons will enable the adults in your class to discover how they can develop the inner character of women and men after God's own heart.

This Course at a Glance

Before you dive into the lessons, familiarize yourself with each lesson's point. Then read the Scripture passages.

- Study them to gain insight into the lessons.
- Use them as a basis for your personal devotions.
- Think about how they relate to people's situations today.

Lesson 1: The Inside Story
The Point: God values inner character more than outer credentials.
Bible Basis: 1 Samuel 16:1-23

Lesson 2: Resisting Evil
The Point: People of character resist their own sinful urges and help others do the same.
Bible Basis: 1 Samuel 25:1-42

Lesson 3: Admitting Sin
The Point: People of character admit their sins and accept God's forgiveness.
Bible Basis: 2 Samuel 12:1-25

Lesson 4: Honoring God
The Point: God honors people of character who seek to honor him.
Bible Basis: 1 Samuel 13:14 and 2 Samuel 7:1-17

PUBLICITY PAGE

Grab your congregation's attention! Add the vital details to the ready-made flier below, photocopy it, and use it to advertise this course on David. Insert the flier in your bulletins. Enlarge it to make posters. Splash the art or anything else from this page in newsletters, in bulletins, or even on postcards! It's that simple.

The art from this page is available on Group's MinistryNet™ on-line resource. Call 800-447-1070 for more information.

A FOUR-WEEK ADULT COURSE ON THE HUMAN CHARACTER OF ISRAEL'S MOST HEROIC KING.

Come to

On

At

Apply·It·To·Life™
Adult
BIBLE CURRICULUM
from Group

COME EXPLORE HOW TO BECOME A PERSON AFTER GOD'S OWN HEART!

The Inside Story

God values inner character more than outer credentials.   ◀ **THE POINT**

OBJECTIVES

Participants will
- compare their inner characteristics to the kingly qualities God values,
- recognize how inaccurate perceptions of others can damage them, and
- commit to developing the inner character of love and service to others.

BIBLE BASIS

Look up the Scripture for this lesson. Then read the following background paragraphs to see how the passage relates to people today.

Saul, Israel's first king, was a huge disappointment. Instead of leading God's people as a king should, Saul let his fear of the people lead him to disobey God and to disgrace himself. Eventually, when Saul rejected God's stated will, God rejected Saul as king over Israel (1 Samuel 15:26). However, this did not signal the end of the Israelite monarchy. On the contrary, it marked the beginning of the reign of Israel's greatest king, David. In 1 Samuel 16:1-23, we discover how David became both the new king and a valued member of the old king's court.

The first 13 verses of the chapter explain how David became king. Simply put, God chose David because he saw something within David that would make him a good king. No one else saw David as God did. Even the prophet Samuel preferred David's older and taller brothers to David. However, God had already given the people their tall king (1 Samuel 8:22; 9:2). This time God was determined to anoint a king for himself (1 Samuel 16:1). That king was David.

The second half of 1 Samuel 16 describes how David, the

1 SAMUEL 16:1-23

newly selected king, entered the royal court. Contrary to what one might expect, David did not assume the reins of power immediately after his anointing. In fact, David entered Saul's service, playing his lyre and providing relief to Saul whenever he was tormented by an evil spirit. In so doing, David revealed himself to be a person of exceptional character.

The two halves of 1 Samuel 16 relate distinct incidents in the life of David, but they are united by a shared theme and theological perspective. The Hebrew root meaning "to see," which appears nine times in the chapter (16:1, 6, 7 [four times], 12, 17, 18), provides the theme of the contrasting ways God and humans look at things. People are often impressed by stature and status (16:6, 7, 17, 18), but God by what he sees in the heart (16:1, 7). Even when we're looking at the same person, we see different things. Nearly everyone who looked at David was struck by his appearance and his expertise with the lyre (16:12, 18, 22). God, however, looked deeply into David's heart and saw a person of integrity and character.

One aspect of that character was revealed in David's reaction to being anointed king, particularly with regard to how he as God's chosen king responded to Saul, God's rejected king. In the first place, the chosen king placed himself at the disposal of the rejected king. Not only did David serve as Saul's armorbearer, he also eased Saul's torment and made Saul's life better. Most people in David's situation would have used Saul's affliction by an evil spirit against him. David, however, used his musical abilities to help Saul by playing the lyre to drive the spirit away whenever it troubled Saul.

As if that were not enough, David also cared about Saul. The Hebrew text of verse 21 literally reads, "David came to Saul, and he presented himself to him, and he loved him, and he became his armorbearer" (see the King James Version and New King James Version). Against the majority of English translations, we should probably conclude that David served Saul out of love for Saul. What God saw in David, then, was a person whose first response to being chosen by God was to love and to serve the one who had rejected God, the one who had been rejected by God.

The original political purpose of 1 Samuel 16 (to defend David's right to the throne) is of little import today, but the chapter's theological concerns are as relevant now as they were then. First, 1 Samuel 16 teaches us that God sees and evaluates people (including ourselves) differently than we do. Unlike most of us, God values inner character more than outer credentials. In addition, 1 Samuel 16 also offers a striking example of the kind of character God esteems. God

chose David to rule as king because he saw in David a capacity and a willingness to love and serve even the one who sat on his (David's) throne. Use this lesson to help your class members appreciate God's interest in inner character and discover what kind of character God values.

THIS LESSON AT A GLANCE

Section	Minutes	What Participants Will Do	Supplies
OPENING	up to 10	**JUDGE AND JURY**—Compare different evaluations of people and learn what today's lesson is about.	
BIBLE EXPLORATION AND APPLICATION	25 to 35	☐ Option 1: **BLUE-RIBBON CHOICE**—Identify the characteristics of a perfect peanut, then read 1 Samuel 16:1-23 to discover the inner qualities God looks for in people.	Bibles, unshelled peanuts, red marker, glue, blue ribbon, pencils, paper, index cards, scissors
	35 to 45	☐ Option 2: **ACCEPT THE REJECTED**—Reject or be rejected, study 1 Samuel 16:1-23 to learn how David loved and accepted Saul, and discuss how to love and accept the rejected today.	Bibles, "Color Clashes" handouts (p. 25), "Accepting the Rejected" handouts (p. 26), red and yellow markers, pins or tape, pencils, scissors
CLOSING	up to 10	**DON'T THROW STONES**—Identify ways to love people instead of "throwing stones" at them, then pray for help in loving people who are difficult to accept.	Small pebbles or stones, plate or shallow bowl
FOR EXTRA TIME	up to 10	**JUDGING A BOOK BY ITS COVER**—Discuss how people misjudge others and how it affects their lives, then apply Matthew 7:1-5 to their own lives.	Bible, several books
	up to 10	**SAUL'S RISE AND DEMISE**—Read 1 Samuel 10:1-13 and 15:1-11, then discuss the role of God's Spirit and the human will in developing inner character.	Bibles

Judge and Jury

(up to 10 minutes)

As participants arrive, invite them to form groups of four. To begin, say: **Think back to your high school days and the people you went to school with.** Pause. **Now, without mentioning names, describe to your group members one person that people generally avoided or rejected.**

When everyone has described someone, ask the entire class the following questions:

- **What was it that made that person someone to avoid?**

- **How might people judge that person differently today?**

- **How do you think God would have viewed that person?**

- **What does this reveal about our values? God's values?**

Say: **We often value others for their physical appearance, their social popularity, or their financial stature. However, God looks at people differently. For the next four weeks we'll be examining the life of David to discover what God values and wants to see in all of us. In the process, we'll discover that David was not only a king of heroic proportions but also a man of human passions, a person we can identify with and learn**

THE **P**OINT▷ **from. We'll start today by discovering that ▷God values inner character more than outer credentials.**

BIBLE **E**XPLORATION
AND **A**PPLICATION

☐ **O**PTION **1**:

Blue-Ribbon Choice

(25 to 35 minutes)

Before class, purchase a bag of peanuts in the shell. Prior to class, carefully open five imperfect or irregularly shaped peanuts. Using a red marker, draw hearts on the peanuts in each of the shells. Then use tacky craft glue, a hot-glue gun, or some other adhesive to glue the shells back together. When the glue dries, mix these peanuts back in with the peanuts in the bag. Cut a 3-inch segment of blue ribbon for every four class members.

Keep people in their groups of four. Have each group choose two members to be Chief Judges and two members to be Field Judges. Give each group a blue ribbon, pencils, and a sheet of paper. Divide the peanuts among the groups.

Say: **Imagine that you're members of a task force whose goal is to find the perfect peanut. Chief Judges, your job is to devise a list of criteria that the perfect peanut must meet. For example, you might decide that it must have perfect color, a smooth shell, and a symmetrical shape. Write your criteria on the paper. While you're doing this, the Field Judges will be sorting through the peanuts and, using their own criteria, dividing them into a "rejected" pile and an "accepted" pile. When the peanuts are divided, the Chief Judges are to use their criteria to choose the perfect peanut from the accepted pile and then award it a blue ribbon.**

Give groups five minutes to make their choices for perfect peanuts. When time is up, have the groups display their blue-ribbon choices. Then ask the entire class the following questions:

- **What criteria did you use to determine which of your peanuts was perfect?**

- **How fully did everyone in your group agree with the criteria you used?**

- **What can you know about the peanut inside by looking at its outer shell?**

Instruct groups to keep the blue-ribbon peanuts for later. Have each group read **1 Samuel 16:1-23.** After everyone has finished, have group members discuss the following questions. Ask the questions one at a time, allowing several minutes for discussion after each one. Ask for volunteers to report their groups' answers after each question. Ask:

- **Why was Samuel's selection for king different from God's?**

- **What criteria did Samuel use in making his choice for king?**

- **What reasons did God give Samuel for choosing David as king?**

- **What were David's outer credentials? inner characteristics?**

- **What does God think of outer credentials? of inner character?**

Say: **In the eyes of many people, David was an unlikely choice for king. He was young, small, without leadership experience, and the son of a shepherd. But God made it clear to Samuel and everyone else that** ▷**he values inner character more than outer creden-**

◁ T H E   P O I N T

You may want to serve extra peanuts and soft drinks or juice to encourage fellowship and fun among your participants. Combining fellowship with teaching is a powerful way to promote community building within your group.

tials. Earlier you selected blue-ribbon peanuts on the basis of various external criteria. But the perfect peanuts are actually those with red hearts drawn on the inside.

Have groups open their blue-ribbon peanuts. Ask people to hold up any peanuts that have red hearts on them. Then have people open up the remaining peanuts to identify all that have the red hearts. Ask the entire class:

● **How are the peanuts with red hearts like the people God chooses to serve him?**

Give everyone an index card and a pencil. Have people write their answers to the following questions. Allow several minutes for people to answer each question. Ask:

● **What outer credentials do people see when they look at you?**

● **What inner character does God see in you that others do not?**

● **How might God use your outer credentials? inner character?**

● **What inner character traits might God want you to develop?**

● **What can you do this week to begin developing those traits?**

T H E   P O I N T ▷

Say: Because ▷God values inner character more than outer credentials, we need to make sure we're developing the inner character traits that he wants us to have. As we do this, God will use both our outer credentials and our inner characteristics in ways that honor and serve him.

■ ■

For *Even Deeper* DISCUSSION

Form groups of four to discuss the following questions.

● Read 1 Samuel 16:1-13. Did Samuel sacrifice as he said he would? If he didn't, did he lie at God's command? Did he deceive? To what extent is it permissible to deceive to accomplish something good?

● Read 1 Samuel 16:1, 7, 12-13 and Psalm 139:13-16. To what extent was God's selection of David based on David's character? on God's free will? How might the nature of a person's heart affect God's choice to use him or her?

● What specific task has God chosen you to do? How has God equipped you to do that? What do you need to do to fulfill God's will for your life?

■ ■

☐ OPTION 2:
Accept the Rejected
(35 to 45 minutes)

Before class, make one photocopy of the "Color Clashes" handout (p. 25) for every six class members. Follow the instructions on the handout. Make one photocopy of the "Accepting the Rejected" handout (p. 26) for each person.

Give each person a card from the "Color Clashes" handout, explaining that the cards will help people form groups for the Bible study that follows. Tell people to secretly read the instructions on the cards and then pin or tape the cards to their shirts with the instructions facing in.

When everyone is wearing a card, say: **Let's form study groups so we can discover in God's Word why God chose a person such as David to be king of all Israel. Follow the instructions on your card to quickly form a group of four.**

Allow people one to two minutes to follow the instructions and to discover that only the Reds can form groups of four. Then get everyone's attention. Address the following questions to the entire class:

- **What's taking some of you so long to find a group?**

- **Reds, why won't you let Yellows join your group?**

- **Yellows, why don't you form a group of your own?**

Say: **The instructions on the cards gave you artificial reasons to reject some people and to accept others. However, rejection and acceptance are real issues we must face every day.** Ask:

- **Yellows, what was it like to be avoided and rejected?**

- **Reds, how did it feel to avoid and reject the Yellows?**

- **How was this like real-life rejection? How was it different?**

- **Why do people in the real world avoid or reject others?**

Say: **People accept and reject each other for various reasons, and sometimes those reasons seem fairly legitimate. For example, when God rejected Saul as king of Israel, David seemed to have good reason to reject Saul as well. After all, David was God's choice to replace Saul. Let's examine 1 Samuel 16 to discover how David and Saul fared during this difficult time.**

Instruct people to form groups of four that contain two Reds and two Yellows. Give each person a copy of the "Accepting the Rejected" handout and a pencil. Tell people to

LESSON 1 ■ 21

read and follow the instructions to complete the top half of the handout.

After 10 minutes, ask for volunteers to report their groups' answers. Then have group members discuss the following questions. After each question, ask for volunteers to summarize their groups' responses. Ask:

- **To what extent did David have a legitimate reason to avoid or reject Saul?**

- **Why did David love and care for Saul even after God had rejected Saul?**

- **What implications does this have for Christians in helping the rejected today?**

THE POINT ▷

TEACHER
TIP

If you're running short of class time, assign each group one of the four categories on the handout, and give groups two minutes to discuss their categories.

THE POINT ▷

Say: **God chose David to replace Saul as king because he knew David had the inner character that would equip him to rule and serve well. Because ▷God values inner character more than outer credentials, our attitudes toward and treatment of others should be shaped by our godly inner character and not their outer characteristics.**

Instruct groups to complete the bottom half of the "Accepting the Rejected" handout. After eight minutes, ask groups to report what they wrote. Then instruct each person to write the answer to the following question on his or her handout. Ask:

- **How will you imitate David by loving and caring for someone who's been rejected?**

Allow people two minutes to write their answers, then say: **God chose David to rule the people of Israel because he had a godly inner character. That character was most evident when David, God's chosen king, loved and served Saul, God's rejected king. Since ▷God values inner character more than outer credentials, we should express the inner character of a loving and serving heart and not avoid or reject people because of their outer characteristics.**

FOR *Even Deeper* DISCUSSION

Form groups of four to discuss the following questions.

- Read 1 Samuel 16:14-15. Why do you think God tormented Saul with an evil spirit? How can a holy God use evil to accomplish his will? What does this imply about God's control of everything? about God's responsibility for everything that happens?

• Since God sent a spirit to torment Saul, was David wrong to relieve Saul's torment? Why or why not? How can we recognize when God is punishing someone? How should we treat people whom God is punishing?

■ ■

Apply·It·To·Life™ This Week! The "Apply-It-To-Life This Week!" handout (p. 27) helps people further explore the issues uncovered in today's class. Give everyone a photocopy of the handout. Encourage class members to take time during the coming week to explore the questions and activities on the handout.

BIBLE INSIGHT

Much of the Old Testament, including 1 Samuel 16:14, was written before many truths regarding Satan and demons were fully revealed. Therefore, the Old Testament generally attributes both good and bad events to God (see Judges 9:23; 1 Kings 22:19-23; Amos 3:6; compare 1 Samuel 24:1 with 1 Chronicles 21:1). By attributing good and bad to God, the Old Testament emphasizes God's absolute control of and ultimate responsibility for all that happens within his creation.

CLOSING

Don't Throw Stones

(up to 10 minutes)

Before class, collect a variety of small stones or pebbles. Place them on a plate or in a shallow bowl. Be sure to have twice as many stones as people in your class.

Instruct everyone to think of someone in his or her family, church, or workplace who is difficult to accept. After 30 seconds, have everyone turn to a partner and describe the person he or she is thinking of, explaining what makes that person hard to accept. People might give reasons related to behavior, attitude, or appearance. Then have each partner tell one way he or she can show more love and acceptance to that person this week.

When everyone is done sharing, form a circle. Pass around the plate of stones so each person can choose his or her favorite stone from the pile. When everyone has a stone, tell people to think about why they chose their stones.

Say: **Just as it's normal to prefer some stones to others, it's natural to like certain people more than others.** Hold up a stone and say: **But when we "throw stones" at others simply because we don't like them or because they don't have the outer characteristics that appeal to us, we dishonor God and damage them. God looks at people's hearts because ▶he values inner character more than outer credentials. As God's children, we should develop the inner character that honors God and accepts others no matter what their outer characteristics may be.**

◀ **THE POINT**

Instruct pairs to close in prayer, thanking God for valuing inner character more than outer credentials and asking God to help everyone develop the inner characteristics of love and acceptance. As people leave, encourage them to take the stones home as a pocket reminder of God's high regard for inner character.

For Extra Time

JUDGING A BOOK BY ITS COVER
(up to 10 minutes)

Hold up several books with which class members will not be familiar. Have people call out words that describe the books and what they think the books are about. After several minutes, ask the entire class the following questions:

- Do you think we've given a fair analysis of the books? Why or why not?
- How is judging a book by its cover like judging people by what we can see of them?
- How do incorrect judgments affect the way we treat people? affect those people?

Read aloud Matthew 7:1-5, then challenge people to look inside each person as God does and to recognize that as Christians we are to accept and love others without prejudging them.

SAUL'S RISE AND DEMISE
(up to 10 minutes)

Form groups of three. Instruct groups to read 1 Samuel 10:1-13 and 15:1-11. Then have groups discuss the following questions. Ask:

- What prompted Saul to prophesy? to disobey God's orders?
- To what extent does God's Spirit enable us to do God's will?
- To what extent can God's Spirit overcome our bad character?
- What is God's role in developing our inner character? What is our responsibility?

Color Clashes

Photocopy and cut apart the cards. Mark the back of the Red group's cards with red marker and the back of the Yellow group's cards with yellow marker.

When you're instructed to form a group of four, avoid people wearing cards with YELLOW on them. Don't speak to, make eye contact with, or acknowledge them in any way.

When you're instructed to form a group of four, seek out only people wearing cards with RED on them. Make every attempt to convince them to join your group.

When you're instructed to form a group of four, avoid people wearing cards with YELLOW on them. Don't speak to, make eye contact with, or acknowledge them in any way.

When you're instructed to form a group of four, seek out only people wearing cards with RED on them. Make every attempt to convince them to join your group.

When you're instructed to form a group of four, avoid people wearing cards with YELLOW on them. Don't speak to, make eye contact with, or acknowledge them in any way.

When you're instructed to form a group of four, seek out only people wearing cards with RED on them. Make every attempt to convince them to join your group.

ACCEPTING the Rejected

As a group, read 1 Samuel 16:1-23 and questions 1 through 4 below. After 10 minutes you'll report your answers to the rest of the class.

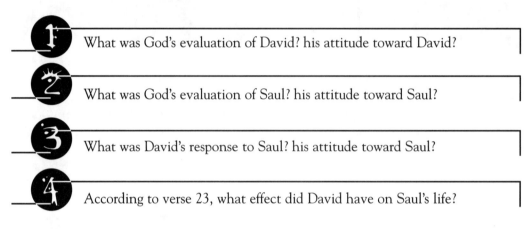

1 What was God's evaluation of David? his attitude toward David?

2 What was God's evaluation of Saul? his attitude toward Saul?

3 What was David's response to Saul? his attitude toward Saul?

4 According to verse 23, what effect did David have on Saul's life?

Identify one group of people that is commonly rejected in each of the areas listed. Then describe ways Christians can follow David's example of loving and caring for each group.

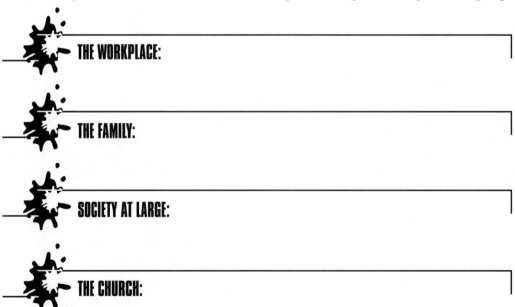

THE WORKPLACE:

THE FAMILY:

SOCIETY AT LARGE:

THE CHURCH:

The Inside Story

God values inner character more
than outer credentials.
1 Samuel 16:1-23

Reflecting on God's Word

Each day this week, read one of the following Scriptures, and examine what it teaches about the characteristics God values. Then consider how you can develop those characteristics in your life. List your discoveries in the space under each passage.

Day 1: 1 Samuel 15:22-23. God prefers obedience to religious acts.

Day 2: Proverbs 6:16-19. God hates everything that promotes conflict.

Day 3: Colossians 3:12-14. God values practical expressions of love.

Day 4: Isaiah 1:16-20. God expects his people to help those who need it.

Day 5: Luke 6:27-36. God wants us to love people who don't love us.

Day 6: 1 Corinthians 1:26-31. God uses people that the world rejects.

Beyond Reflection

Read a newspaper or magazine to identify individuals or groups of people who seem to be avoided, rejected, or oppressed. List the individuals and groups, then pray for them, asking God to help you and others be more tolerant and accepting of all people. Think of one way you can show God's love and acceptance to one of the groups, and commit to doing that deed sometime during the next few weeks.

Coming Next Week: Resisting Evil (1 Samuel 25:1-42)

Resisting Evil

People of character resist their own sinful urges and help others do the same.

◀ **THE POINT**

OBJECTIVES

Participants will
- recognize the long-term consequences of impulsive actions,
- explore how David and Abigail responded to David's evil urge, and
- commit to resisting negative impulses whenever they can.

BIBLE BASIS

Look up the Scripture for this lesson. Then read the following background paragraphs to see how the passage relates to people today.

Many years passed before God's appointment of David as king of Israel became a political reality (compare 1 Samuel 16:1-13 with 2 Samuel 2:1-4a; 5:1-5). Although David possessed God's Spirit, the love of Saul's children, continual military success, the adoration of all Israel, and the presence of God (1 Samuel 18:1-9, 12, 20, 28-30), Saul still held the reins of political power. In fact, although David loved and served Saul without fail, Saul feared and resented David so much that he tried to kill him on several occasions (1 Samuel 18:10-13; 19:9-10; 20:32-33). To save his life, David eventually fled Saul's palace to live in the foreign lands and wilderness areas surrounding Israel (1 Samuel 21:1–30:31).

During this time, the contrast between David as God's leader and Saul as Israel's king demonstrated an important truth, that human reality and divine reality are often not the same. That is, Saul commanded the political position, but David possessed the divine power. Furthermore, because David recognized that political reality and theological reality aren't always the same, he resisted his ambitions and waited

1 SAMUEL 25:1-42

BIBLE INSIGHT

for God to establish him as divinely appointed leader and politically authorized king.

David was human, however, and sometimes the gap between his high expectations and the hard realities of his situation frustrated him. For example, 1 Samuel 25:1-42 describes a time David nearly surrendered to an urge to avenge his wounded honor. The account of David's struggle with and eventual victory over this desire shows us how people of character respond to sinful impulses whenever they experience or encounter them.

The main characters in the story offer different examples of good and evil character. Nabal, for example, plays the villain who repays good with evil (verses 15, 21). David, by way of contrast, initially seeks to return evil for evil (verses 17, 39) but eventually rejects his evil impulse in favor of God's good promise (verses 28, 30-31). Abigail is revealed to be the most praiseworthy of the three characters, for she risks personal harm to save her husband and her household from David's evil plan (verses 24-31, 34). Finally, to bring the story to a fitting conclusion, God vindicates David's honor and rewards his faith by returning Nabal's evil upon Nabal himself (verses 38-39).

The narrator of 1 Samuel 25 uses these characters and their experiences to teach a number of truths. For example, we learn from Nabal that people who follow their evil impulses may receive from God the very evil they direct against others. Moreover, we see in David that even people of good character struggle with evil impulses. Both David and Nabal feel sinful impulses, but David reveals his moral superiority by resisting the temptation to do wrong. Finally, Abigail teaches us that sometimes we should risk our own comfort and safety for the sake of a greater good.

According to 1 Samuel 25:1-42, good character shows itself in several ways. Sometimes it enables us to control our passions long enough to consider the consequences of following an impulse. At other times good character leads us to help others understand why they should resist their sinful urges. In either case, we can learn from David and Abigail how people of character resist their own evil urges and help others do the same.

Although spontaneity can spice up a dull existence, not every spontaneous act is good or godly. Use this lesson to help your class members discover how to evaluate impulses and to resist those that are bad. In so doing, you will help them develop the kind of character that honors God and benefits others.

Section	Minutes	What Participants Will Do	Supplies
OPENING	up to 10	**IT'S HUMAN NATURE**—Discuss times they felt wronged or insulted to discover that everyone feels the urge to retaliate.	
BIBLE EXPLORATION AND APPLICATION	25 to 35	☐ Option 1: **WHY RESIST?**—Compete to avoid an unpleasant outcome, study 1 Samuel 25:1-42 to discover why they shouldn't win at others' expense, and apply what they learned to their competition and to their own situations.	Bibles, "Resist the Urge" handouts (p. 40), newspapers, markers, pencils
	30 to 40	☐ Option 2: **ON A WHIM**—Make impulsive choices they might regret and learn from 1 Samuel 25:1-42 how they can resist bad urges and help others do likewise.	Bibles, "On a Whim" handout (p. 41), colored markers, paper, pencils, marker, newsprint, scissors, tape
CLOSING	up to 10	**BLESSED ARE THE PEACEMAKERS**—Discover God's promise to peacemakers and pray for help to be peacemakers in their own situations.	Bible, index cards, pencils
FOR EXTRA TIME	up to 10	**STEP UP TO BAT**—Discuss current events that illustrate sinful impulses and list strategies and boundaries for intervening in difficult situations.	
	up to 10	**AN URGENT URGE**—Decide whether various urges are good or bad and discuss how resisting and acting on urges might affect themselves and others.	

It's Human Nature

(up to 10 minutes)

Say: **Welcome to the second week of our study on the life and character of David. Last week we learned that God chose David to replace Saul as king of Israel because God values inner character more than outer credentials. During the rest of our study on David, we'll examine incidents in David's life to discover the kind of inner character God saw in David and wants to see in each of us. To get us started today, turn to someone other than your spouse, and tell about a time you felt someone wronged or insulted you.**

After several minutes, have partners answer the following questions:

- **What emotions did the wrong or insult evoke in you?**

- **How did you want to respond or react to the insult?**

Then ask everyone who felt at least a little urge to retaliate or to seek revenge to raise a hand. Instruct people to look around the room at the raised hands. Then ask the entire class:

- **What do all the raised hands reveal about the human tendency to want revenge?**

Say: **Sometimes people think that, if they were truly good, they wouldn't feel the urge to do bad things. But even people of good and godly character experience evil impulses. Still, just because we all have sinful urges doesn't mean that it's OK to follow them. Today we'll learn from an event in the life of David that ▷people of character resist their sinful urges and help others do the same.**

THE POINT ▷

☐ **OPTION 1:**

Why Resist?

(25 to 35 minutes)

Before class, make one photocopy of the "Resist the Urge" handout (p. 40) for each class member.

Clear a large space in the middle of your classroom. Set chairs across the center of the room to divide the space into two halves. Instruct people to number off by twos to form two teams. Have the Ones stand on one side of the center line and the Twos on the other side. Instruct each team to select a leader, then call the two leaders aside. Quietly tell the leaders they are to act as peacemakers later in the activity. Explain that they are to intervene if someone on the winning team attempts to draw a dot on the nose of a losing team member.

Give team members each a sheet of newspaper, and instruct them to crumple the papers. Then say: **Let's begin our time with a short game of missile war. The object of this game is to throw paper missiles into the other team's territory until I call time. The team that ends up with the fewest missiles on its side is the winning team. There are two rules. You can't throw paper missiles directly at people, and** (hold up a marker) **members of the winning team will draw dots on the noses of people on the losing team.**

Begin the game, then call time after 30 seconds. Count the paper missiles on each side to determine the winning team. If teams tie, play additional 30-second rounds until one team wins.

Say: **In a few minutes, we'll let the winning team draw dots on the noses of the losing team members. But first I'd like us to look at an incident in David's life that has a lot to teach us about winning and losing.**

Form groups of four that contain two members of the winning team and two members of the losing team. Give each person a copy of the "Resist the Urge" handout and a pencil. Instruct people to read and follow the instructions at the top of the handout.

After 10 minutes, ask for volunteers to report their groups' discoveries. Then say: **One of the rules of our prior competition was that the winners would draw dots on the noses of the losers. Let's have the winners stand up.** Hand several markers to members of the winning team. Say: **Use these markers to bring our competition to a successful conclusion.** Pause for any responses or objections. If the people with the markers attempt to draw dots, have the peacemakers you chose earlier intervene. Encourage them to help the winners resist their urge to draw on the losers' noses by explaining why doing so would be a poor choice.

Gather the class. Then ask the entire class the following questions:

- **How did you feel about drawing on someone's nose? about having your nose drawn on?**

- **What would the winners have gained by drawing dots? What would they have lost?**

TEACHER TIP

If you have a significant number of class members who might be uncomfortable throwing paper wads, use some other competitive activity. For example, have people stand 10 feet from a coffee can or plastic container and take turns trying to toss pennies into the container. The team with the most pennies in the container would be the winning team. Make sure you announce before you begin play that the winning team will draw dots on the noses of the losing team.

- What did the winners lose by resisting the urge to draw dots? What did they gain?

- How did waiting to draw on the losers' noses make it easier to resist the urge to do so?

Say: **In real life, our urges to win at the expense of others are probably not as serious as David's nor as silly as our competition's. However, we all face situations in which we need to resist the impulse to win at any cost.**

Have people re-form their original groups of four and discuss the following questions. After each question, ask for volunteers to report their groups' responses. Ask:

- **In what ways do we try to "win" in our relationships with others?**

- **How does winning at someone else's expense harm others? ourselves?**

- **How might resisting a harmful urge to win benefit others? ourselves?**

- **How can God help us resist the urge to win at someone else's expense?**

Instruct people to write the answers to the two questions that follow on their handouts. Ask:

- **When do you most often feel an urge to win at someone else's expense?**

- **What should you do to resist that harmful urge the next time it arises?**

Say: **There's nothing wrong with winning. However, when we harm people in an attempt to benefit ourselves, our long-term losses are usually greater than our short-term gains. So whenever we feel the urge to win at another person's expense, we need to remind ourselves that ▷people of character resist their own sinful urges and help others do the same.**

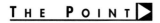 T H E P O I N T ▷

██████████████████████████

For *Even Deeper* Discussion

Form groups of four to discuss the following questions:

- What's the difference between seeking revenge and standing up for our rights? When should we stand up for our rights? give up our rights? What are the benefits of standing up for our rights? of giving up our rights?

- Read Nahum 1:2-3 and Hebrews 10:30-31. When, if ever, is it permissible to seek revenge? to ask God for vengeance?

How should God's promise to punish the guilty affect the way we respond when people wrong us? when we wrong others?

■■■■■■■■■■■■■■■■■■■■■■■■■

☐ OPTION 2:

On a Whim

(30 to 40 minutes)

Before class, make one photocopy of the "On a Whim" handout (p. 41) for every eight class members. You'll need one card for each person. Use markers to draw a design such as a heart, a star, polka dots, stripes, a flower, or a diamond on the back of each card. You may repeat the designs as needed, but vary the colors of repeated designs.

Place the cards on a table with the designs facing up. Be sure that you have at least as many cards as you have people in class.

Say: **Many of us admire people who feel free enough to act spontaneously. Taking flowers home on a whim or buying a surprise treat for the kids is a delight that never grows old. So let's take a moment to be spontaneous. I've laid out various cards on this table. Each card has a task that I'll ask you to perform a little later. You have five seconds to choose a card and return to your seat. Keep your card face down at all times so you see only the colorful design. Go!**

When everyone has a card, ask the entire class the following questions:

● **Why did you select the particular card that you did?**

● **What would make your choice a good one? a bad one?**

Say: **Being spontaneous is often exhilarating and exciting, but sometimes our impulses lead us to decisions and actions that we later regret. For example, some of you will probably wish you had chosen a different card when you read what's written on the back of the card you selected.**

Pause for 15 seconds, then instruct people to turn over their cards and read what's written on the other side. Allow people time to read and to react to their instructions. Then tell people to stand and do what's written on their cards.

When everyone who wants to has followed the instructions, have people form groups of four to discuss the following questions:

● **How did you feel about having to make an impulsive choice?**

TEACHER
TIP

Unless you have a very animated group, you'll probably have only a few people brave enough to perform the actions. That's OK—the activity will still help people experience how impulsive choices sometimes produce unwanted consequences.

BIBLE
INSIGHT

By going out to meet David, Abigail was placing herself in a precarious position. She was disobeying her husband's decision not to give food to David and his men (verses 9-11) and also risking her life by standing between David and her husband (verse 34). David recognized, however, that God sent Abigail to keep David from shedding blood (verses 32-33). Abigail was following God's will when she sent food to David and convinced him to turn back. On two other occasions, David followed God's will in a similar manner by convincing his warriors not to kill Saul even though they had the chance to do so (1 Samuel 24:1-7; 26:7-11).

THE POINT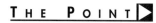

● **What did you think of your choice after you read your card?**

● **How is this choice like impulsive choices in real life? How is it different?**

Say: **Because our impulses and urges aren't always reliable, we need to learn how to recognize bad impulses and then respond to them with good choices. Let's examine an event in the life of David that gives us insight into how we can do that.**

Form groups of four. Have group members read together **1 Samuel 25:1-42.** When groups finish reading, instruct group members to answer the following questions. Allow groups two minutes to discuss each question, then have volunteers report their groups' responses. Ask:

● **To what extent was David wrong to feel an urge to retaliate? to act on his urge?**

● **How was Abigail's impulse to intervene like David's urge to retaliate? How was it different?**

● **How did Abigail help David resist his vengeful impulse?**

● **What steps did David take to resist his initial impulse?**

● **How did God honor David's eventual rejection of his urge?**

Say: **We can see from this story that personal character takes various forms. At times ▷people of character resist their own sinful urges; at times they help others resist their bad impulses. Therefore, as people of character, sometimes we need to follow the example of David and sometimes the example of Abigail.**

Give each group a sheet of paper and a pencil. Assign half the groups David and half Abigail. Instruct the David groups to list all the principles we can learn from David about how to resist our evil urges. Direct the Abigail groups to list all the principles we learn from Abigail about how to help others resist their sinful impulses.

While groups are discussing, hang two sheets of newsprint where everyone can see them. Write "David" at the top of one sheet and "Abigail" at the top of the other. After five minutes, ask groups to report their principles to the rest of the class. Record their ideas on the newsprint.

When groups finish reporting, instruct everyone to think of a situation in which he or she, like David, has felt a sinful urge. Then have people turn to partners, briefly describe the situation, and tell how they will resist the urge in the future.

After several minutes, have everyone think of a situation in which he or she, like Abigail, might help someone resist an evil urge. Then have people describe the situation to their partners (without mentioning names) and tell how they will help those people resist the sinful urges in the future.

After a few minutes, say: **We can be spontaneous without being dangerous when we become ▶people of character who resist our own sinful urges and help others do the same. So when we're tempted by a harmful urge or see someone else struggle with a negative impulse, let's follow the examples of David and Abigail and respond to those bad urges with good choices and good advice.**

◀ THE POINT

■ ■

For *Even Deeper* Discussion

Form groups of four to discuss the following questions:

● How should we balance our responsibility as Christian peacemakers against people's right to make their own decisions? When, if ever, should we use physical force to compel others to resist their sinful urges? To what extent should we support laws that keep people from acting on their sinful urges?

● Read Proverbs 12:20 and 22:3. Was Abigail wise or foolish to place herself between David and her husband? To what extent was it right for Abigail to give food to David after her husband had refused it? What can Abigail teach us about putting ourselves at risk to keep others from doing evil?

■ ■

Apply·It·To·Life™ *This Week!* The "Apply-It-To-Life This Week!" handout (p. 42) helps people further explore the issues uncovered in today's class. Give everyone a photocopy of the handout. Encourage class members to take time during the coming week to explore the questions and activities on the handout.

CLOSING

Blessed Are the Peacemakers

(up to 10 minutes)

Keep people in their groups of four. Give an index card to each person and a pencil to anyone who needs one.

THE POINT ▷

Say: **God wants us to promote peaceful relations whenever and however we can. In fact, Jesus promised a specific blessing to ▷people of character who actively work for peace by resisting their own sinful urges and by helping others do the same.**

Read **Matthew 5:9.** Then ask people to write the verse on their cards while you slowly read through it several more times.

Then say: **As God's children, we can follow the examples of David and Abigail to "make peace" in our relationships with others and in their dealings with one another. Think of a situation in your life in which you need to act as a peacemaker. For example, you may need to resist your own evil urge to make a cutting remark, or you might need to help someone else resist a negative impulse.**

Allow 30 seconds of reflection time, then instruct people to write on their cards what they will do to act as a peacemaker in the situation. After several minutes, have group members briefly share what they will do to act as peacemakers. Then have group members close by praying for each other, asking God to give them the wisdom and the courage to act as peacemakers whenever and however they can.

Encourage people to take their index cards home as a reminder to promote God's peace by resisting their own sinful urges and by helping others do the same.

🕐 *For Extra Time*

STEP UP TO BAT
(up to 10 minutes)

Ask people to describe recent local or national events that illustrate social and moral evils such as violence, discrimination, deceit, and theft. Then form small groups. Assign an event to each group. Then have group members discuss the following questions in relation to acting as God's peacemakers in the world. Ask:

- **To what extent was the incident produced by someone's sinful impulse?**

- **What were the short-term results of the incident? the long-term consequences?**

- **To what extent could someone have intervened to prevent the incident?**

- **If you were there, how would you have worked to promote God's peace?**

TEACHER TIP

You may want to cut out and bring to class newspaper and magazine articles that deal with these social and moral evils. Then ask different persons to read the articles to the rest of the class.

AN URGENT URGE
(up to 10 minutes)

Ask people to form groups of three or four. Instruct groups to brainstorm the likely implications of acting on the following urges. Groups should discuss why the urge may be good or bad and then list the consequences of resisting and of acting on the urge.

- the urge to cut off or honk at a bad driver
- the urge to eat some or all of a chocolate cake
- the urge to cheat on your income taxes
- the urge to bring flowers to a co-worker you've argued with
- the urge to talk about a friend in your neighborhood
- the urge to leave work early when your supervisor is gone
- the urge to cook a special meal for your family

Resist the URGE

As a group, read 1 Samuel 25:1-42 and the information in the FYI box. Then answer the questions below. After 10 minutes you'll have the chance to report your insights to the rest of the class.

● How legitimate was David's anger with Nabal? his plan to destroy Nabal?

_____

● Why do you think Abigail intervened in the conflict between David and Nabal?

_____

● What would David have won by destroying Nabal?

_____

_____

● What did David gain by resisting his urge to destroy Nabal?

_____

_____

On a Whim

Take off your shoes, and tiptoe around the room singing ... "I'm a Little Teapot."

Hold your nose and sing ... "Frère Jacques."

Hop around the room like a kangaroo while you moo like a cow.

Wave your socks in the air.

Hop around the room saying "Ooo-ooo-ooo" like a monkey.

Touch your finger to your nose.

Do three somersaults at the front of the room. 1-2-3, here I go!

Skip around the room with your eyes closed. Close those eyes!

Apply·It·To·Life™
This Week!

Resisting Evil

People of character resist their own sinful urges and help others do the same.

1 Samuel 25:1-42

Reflecting on God's Word

Each day this week, read one of the following Scriptures, and examine what it teaches about acting with vengeance or forgiveness. Then consider how to develop the inner qualities of a peacemaker in your life. List your discoveries in the space under each passage.

Day 1: Leviticus 19:17-18. We should correct others but never stop loving them.

Day 2: Matthew 6:7-14. God honors a forgiving spirit more than a wordy prayer.

Day 3: Deuteronomy 32:34-43. God will act justly to vindicate his people.

Day 4: Ephesians 4:31–5:2. We should replace feelings of anger with acts of love.

Day 5: Romans 12:9-21. God commands us to overcome evil with good deeds.

Day 6: 1 Thessalonians 5:13-22. We should live in peace and avoid every evil.

Beyond Reflection

Watch a few popular television shows and evaluate the various urges or impulses represented. Answer the following questions for each show:
- Which of the impulses are positive? Which are negative?
- How do the characters in the show respond to their impulses?
- How should the characters react when they feel these urges?
- How are these TV situations like those you face in real life?
- How will you promote good urges in your life? good responses to sinful urges?

Coming Next Week: Admitting Sin (2 Samuel 12:1-25)

Admitting Sin

P eople of character admit their sins and accept God's forgiveness.

OBJECTIVES

Participants will
- discover that even people of character give in to sinful urges,
- learn from David how to admit sin and accept forgiveness, and
- apply what they learn by dealing with the sin in their lives.

BIBLE BASIS

Look up the Scripture for this lesson. Then read the following background paragraphs to see how the passage relates to people today.

Many years after God had appointed David to replace Saul as king of Israel, Saul was killed in battle against the Philistines (1 Samuel 31:1-7), and David took his place on the throne (2 Samuel 2:1-7; 5:1-5). David's rise to power was neither smooth nor speedy, and men such as Jonathan, Abner, and Ish-Bosheth lost their lives in the process (1 Samuel 31:1-7; 2 Samuel 3:22-39; 4:1-12). However, David displayed his moral integrity by keeping his hands unstained by blood and by actually mourning the deaths of the men who opposed him.

David believed that God would make him king at the right time, so he rejected political intrigues that might expedite his ascent to the throne. David realized that the end doesn't justify the means even when the end is the promise and the will of God, so he patiently waited for God to make him king. God, for his part, honored David's faith and character by enabling David to establish Jerusalem as his political and religious capital, to subdue the Philistines once and for all, to extend Israel's borders in every direction, and to turn back

2 SAMUEL 12:1-25

every threat against his rule and realm (2 Samuel 5:6-10; 6:12-15; 8:1-14; 10:1-19).

God so blessed David that he appeared impregnable. By the end of 2 Samuel 10, there were no visible chinks in David's military strength or in his moral character. But the scandalous events of 2 Samuel 11 shattered that image of David and shook his kingdom to its very core. David, the king after God's own heart, committed adultery with Bathsheba (verses 1-5) and then had Uriah, her husband, killed in battle (verses 6-25). Just when David appeared free from danger, he undermined his own rule by sinning against the God who had made him king. For the rest of his days, David lived with the consequences of his actions as he watched his family and his kingdom crumble from within (2 Samuel 13–21). Ironically, David was a greater threat to himself than any external enemy had ever been. From this we learn that the greatest threat to God's people is internal rather than external, the threat that our own sins introduce into our midst.

Because David initially excused Uriah's death with a proverb about "the sword" (2 Samuel 11:25), God decreed that "the sword" would never depart from David's family (12:9-11). In the years that followed, David's son Amnon raped his own half-sister Tamar (13:1-22), Absalom (Tamar's full brother) murdered Amnon (13:23-39), and Absalom died in his attempt to overthrow his own father, David (15:1–18:33).

Within the context of this negative time of David's life, 2 Samuel 12:1-25 depicts his positive example of dealing with sin in the proper way. God set the process in motion by confronting David with his sin. Because David had acted as though nothing had happened, God sent the prophet Nathan to trap David with a story about a stolen lamb. When David declared that the thief should die, Nathan informed David that he was the "thief" and that God was going to punish his secret sins in the sight of all Israel. David's response to Nathan's revelation was simple but pivotal: "I have sinned against the Lord" (verse 13). David admitted his guilt without qualification or excuse.

When David honestly admitted his sins, God commuted the death sentence that David had unwittingly pronounced upon himself (verse 5). However, God did not let David's sins go unpunished. Instead, he transferred David's penalty to David and Bathsheba's infant son and kept intact the other punishments Nathan had announced. David pleaded with God to let his son live, but eventually the child died. At this point David's inner character revealed itself. Although David had begged God not to go through with the punishment, he accepted it when God's will became clear (verses 15b-23).

Finally, after admitting his sins and accepting his punishment, David acknowledged God's forgiveness by going on with life. Instead of dwelling on the past, David dealt with the reality of the present. David and Bathsheba's son was dead, so David comforted Bathsheba and filled the void as much as possible with another child, Solomon (verses 24-25). Although David could never completely escape the consequences of his sin, he could try to repair the damage and rebuild his life. God approved of David's resolve and eventually used Solomon to sustain David's dynasty in Israel (1 Kings 1:38-40; 2:1-12).

People of character aren't perfect. Like everyone else, they sometimes give in to evil impulses and sin against God and others. What sets people of character apart is that they admit their sins and accept God's forgiveness on God's terms. Use this lesson to help your class members develop the inner character that will please God even when their actions don't.

THIS LESSON AT A GLANCE

Section	Minutes	What Participants Will Do	Supplies
OPENING	*up to 10*	**GO AHEAD—ADMIT IT!**—Discuss times they have admitted being wrong, have been punished for sin, or have needed to forgive themselves.	
BIBLE EXPLORATION AND APPLICATION	*25 to 35*	☐ *Option 1:* **BALANCING ACT**—Compare the difficulty of balancing beans to living without sin, then examine 2 Samuel 12:1-25 to discover how David dealt with his sins.	Bibles, "Dealing With Sin" handouts (p. 53), dry beans, craft sticks, pencils
	30 to 40	☐ *Option 2:* **SPILL THE BEANS**—Try to cover their "sins," then study 2 Samuel 12:1-25 to discover how David responded to God's exposure of his sins.	Bibles, "Spill the Beans" handouts (p. 54), dry red beans, white correction fluid, pencils
CLOSING	*up to 10*	**THE FORGIVENESS CIRCLE**—Review how sin pushes us away from God and how dealing with sin draws us closer to God.	
FOR EXTRA TIME	*up to 10*	**NO COMPARISON**—Read 1 Samuel 13:1-15 and 15:1-31, then compare how David and Saul dealt with their sins and how God responded to each man.	Bibles
	up to 10	**AVOIDANCE TECHNIQUES**—Define, role play, and discuss techniques they use to avoid admitting sin.	Index cards, pencil

Go Ahead—Admit It!

(up to 10 minutes)

Form trios. Have trio members number off by threes. Instruct trio members to discuss the following questions, having the Ones answer the first group of questions, the Twos the second group, and so on. Allow approximately two minutes for people to answer each set of questions. Ask:

- **Ones, when have you had to admit you were wrong? How did you admit your mistake? How did admitting a mistake make you feel?**

- **Twos, when have you been punished for something you did? How did you feel about being punished? How well did you accept the punishment?**

- **Threes, when have you needed to forgive yourself? Why did you need to do this? How easy was it to forgive yourself and go on with life?**

After the Threes answer their questions, ask the entire class the following questions:

- **What do our experiences reveal about the pervasiveness of sin? the consequences of sin?**

Say: **The Bible clearly states that everyone since Adam and Eve has sinned and fallen short of God's perfect standard. And just as Adam and Eve tried to cover their shame with fig leaves, we try to hide our sins from God, others, and ourselves with rationalizations, justifications, denials, and outright lies. But it's impossible to hide anything from our all-seeing God, and sooner or later we'll have to deal with every sin. So today we're going to learn from the story of David's sin with Bathsheba how ▷ people of character admit their sins and accept God's forgiveness.**

THE POINT ▷

TEACHER TIP

If you can't find craft sticks, plastic spoons will also work, and have adults balance their beans on the spoon handles. In addition, you may give each person fewer beans, but make sure that people have more beans than they can easily carry on a craft stick or plastic spoon handle.

BIBLE EXPLORATION AND APPLICATION

□ **OPTION 1:**

Balancing Act

(25 to 35 minutes)

Before class, make one photocopy of the "Dealing With Sin" handout (p. 53) for each class member.

Give each person five dry pinto or red beans and a craft stick. Say: **Let's have a little fun today with a balancing act. I want you to line up at the end of the room with your beans balanced on your stick. Your challenge is to walk across the room, touch the opposite wall, and return to the starting place without dropping a bean. If a bean falls off, pick it up, return to the starting place, and begin again. You have one minute to complete the course.**

Begin the activity. Continue for one minute or until everyone has successfully completed the course. Then ask the entire class the following questions:

- **How is the challenge of balancing beans like the difficulty of living sin-free? How is it different?**

- **What was negative about starting over each time you dropped a bean? What was positive about it?**

- **How is the penalty for dropping a bean like the consequences of our sins? How is it different?**

Say: **Probably everyone here struggles to resist temptation and remain as sin-free as possible. However, just as every one of us would eventually drop a bean if we played long enough, every one of us will inevitably give in to a sinful urge. Even David, a person after God's own heart, surrendered to his sinful urge to steal another man's wife. Let's examine this incident to discover how David dealt with his sins of adultery and murder.**

Instruct people to form three groups. If you have more than 18 people in your class, form multiple groups of six or fewer people. Give each person a copy of the "Dealing With Sin" handout and a pencil. Assign the "Admitting Sin," "Accepting Punishment," and "Acknowledging Forgiveness" sections of the handout to different groups. Instruct groups to follow the instructions at the top of the handout.

After about seven minutes, ask people to summarize their groups' insights for the rest of the class. Encourage people to record other groups' discoveries on their handouts.

Then say: **We see in this story that David took three steps to deal with his sins. First, David honestly admitted his sins. Then he accepted God's punishment for his actions. Finally, he acknowledged God's forgiveness so he could begin to rebuild his life.**

Have group members answer the following questions. After each question, ask for volunteers to report their groups' responses. Ask:

- **Can we admit our sins without accepting God's punishment? Explain.**

TEACHER TIP

If your group is too large for people to compete individually, modify this activity into a relay. Form several lines that stretch from one side of the room to the other. Then have people pass the sticks with the beans on them down the line and back. If a bean drops, have the group return the bean and stick to the head of the line and begin passing again.

BIBLE INSIGHT

Psalm 51 conveys more fully David's repentant attitude at this time. In this psalm David assumes complete responsibility for the sin (verses 3-5), begs God to cleanse him from his guilt (verses 1-2, 5-9), and asks God to help him live sin-free in the future (verses 10-12). In return, David promises to teach others from his experience (verses 13-14) and to praise God for his goodness (verses 15-19).

- How does accepting punishment help us acknowledge God's forgiveness?

- How can the knowledge of God's forgiveness help us forgive ourselves?

THE POINT ▷

Say: **When God confronted David with his sins, ▷David revealed himself to be a person of character by admitting his sins and by accepting God's forgiveness on God's terms. As we apply what we've learned from David to our lives, we will become people of character too.**

Instruct people to think of a sin in their lives for which they need to make confession, accept punishment, or acknowledge forgiveness. Direct people to write on the back of their handouts which of the three steps they most need to take: admitting the sin, accepting the punishment, or acknowledging God's forgiveness. Then have people write what they will do during the coming week to take that step. Allow approximately a minute for people to write, then instruct people to list the likely benefits of dealing with that sin.

After approximately a minute, have group members pray for each other, asking God to help all of them admit their sins, accept his punishment, and acknowledge his forgiveness.

After people finish praying, say: **Just as David accepted God's punishment and forgiveness for his sinful deeds, we can live with the certainty that God can and will remove our sins if we act as ▷people of character who admit their sins and accept God's forgiveness on God's terms.**

THE POINT ▷

■ ■

FOR *Even Deeper* DISCUSSION

Form groups of four to discuss the following questions.

- Read 2 Samuel 12:13-14. Did God punish David and Bathsheba's child for David's sins? Explain. What does this reveal about the difference between human ideas of fairness and God's standards of justice?

- God punished David for his secret sins by shaming him in public (2 Samuel 12:11-12; 16:20-22). When should private sins be exposed publicly? Who should expose the sins? What should be the goal of such public exposure of sins?

- To what extent does God view all sins as equally wrong? To what extent does God punish all sins equally? Should we view all sins as the same? Explain. Should we punish all sins in the same way? Explain.

■ ■

☐ **O P T I O N   2 :**

Spill the Beans

(30 to 40 minutes)

Before class, make one photocopy of the "Spill the Beans" handout (p. 54) for each class member. You'll also need white correction fluid and a bag of dry red beans. Prior to class, paint one bean completely white for each person.

Form groups of four. Give each person a white bean and each group 20 red beans. Say: **The white bean you're holding represents the incriminating evidence of a sin you've committed. When I say "go," pile your beans on the floor and work to hide the damaging evidence with the red beans. You'll have 30 seconds to cover your doleful deed. Ready? Go!**

After 30 seconds, call time. Many beans should be partially visible or completely uncovered. Say: **Hmm—it appears that you haven't managed to hide your sins. You still have pieces of incriminating evidence showing. The verdict?** Pause. **Guilty as charged! Your sentence will be handed down a little later.**

Ask the entire class the following questions:

● **How did it feel to try to completely cover your white beans?**

● **How did adding beans help you cover the evidence? hinder you?**

● **How is this activity like trying to hide our sins with more sins?**

● **How fully can we hide our sins from human sight? from God's sight?**

Say: **When we sin, our first tendency is often to hide our awful actions and dispose of any damaging evidence. We often respond to sin by covering it with even greater wrong. But responding to sin in the right way can be just as important as resisting our sinful urges in the first place. So let's explore how David responded to his sinful relationship with Bathsheba and how he reacted to God's punishment of his sin.**

Give each person a copy of the "Spill the Beans" handout and a pencil. Have group members complete the handout together.

After 10 minutes, ask for volunteers to report their groups' insights to the rest of the class. Then have group members discuss the following questions. Ask:

● **How do we try to hide our sins from others? from ourselves? from God?**

● **What happens when we try to hide our sins with even more sin?**

T E A C H E R

If you didn't complete Option 1, explain to people during the report time the three steps of dealing with sin: admitting our sins, accepting God's punishment, and acknowledging God's forgiveness by getting on with our lives. You may wish to write the three steps on a sheet of newsprint taped to the wall so people can refer to them in the application questions that follow.

● **What means does God use to expose our sins to ourselves? to others?**

● **In what specific ways should we respond when God reveals our sins?**

Have people silently answer the following questions. Invite people to write their answers on their handouts. Pause one minute after asking each question. Ask:

● **How have you been trying to hide sin in your life?**

● **What steps should you take to deal with that sin?**

T H E   P O I N T ▷

Say: **David learned that trying to cover sin with more sin only compounds the problem. Fortunately, although God hates our sins, he loves us even when we sin. That's why God uncovers our sins and invites us to admit our guilt, accept our punishment, and then acknowledge his forgiveness by going on with our lives. Because David was ▷ a person of character, he admitted his sins and accepted God's forgiveness on God's terms. As we follow David's positive example, we'll grow in character.**

Now for the sentencing from our earlier bean activity: Each of you must carry your white bean to remind you that God forgives us when we "spill the beans" to him by admitting our sin and accepting his forgiveness.

■ ■

FOR *Even Deeper* DISCUSSION

Form groups of four to discuss the following questions.

● A convicted mass-murderer in prison claims to have admitted his sin and accepted God's forgiveness, and he wants to market his conversion story. To what extent should we forgive the murderer? support his ministry? What does forgiveness require of us? What does it not require of us?

● A pastor confesses to an adulterous affair with someone in the congregation. Should the pastor be allowed to remain at the church? in ministry at another church? What if the pastor confesses to several affairs? Should we punish Christian leaders more or less severely than others who commit the same sin? Explain.

■ ■

Apply·It·To·Life™
This Week!
The "Apply-It-To-Life This Week!" handout (p. 55) helps people further explore the issues uncovered in today's class. Give everyone a photocopy of the handout. Encourage class

members to take time during the coming week to explore the questions and activities on the handout.

The Forgiveness Circle

(up to 10 minutes)

Have people stand in a tight circle and join hands. Say: **Let's conclude today's lesson by silently reflecting on what we've learned. Close your eyes and think of a sin you've committed.** Pause. **How do you feel about what you've done?** Pause. **How do you think God feels about your sin?** Pause.

Now let's open our eyes and face the consequences of our sin. Because God is holy, sin pushes us away from him. Take one step backward to show how your sin separates you from God. Pause. **Sin also leads us to create walls behind which we try to hide from God. Take another step backward to show how your sin builds barriers between God and you.** Pause. **Finally, one sin often leads to more sins as we justify, rationalize, deny, and lie in a futile effort to cover our deeds. Take one step backward to show how sin breeds more sin.** Pause.

But God loves us so much that he's provided a way for us to deal with our sins. We begin by admitting to God and ourselves that we were wrong. Take one step forward to show how admitting your sin will draw you nearer to God. Pause. **When we honestly admit our sins, we're able to accept God's discipline. Take one step forward to show how accepting the consequences of your actions will teach you not to repeat your error.** Pause. **Finally, when we admit our sins and accept our correction, we can enjoy God's forgiveness. Take one step forward to show how acknowledging God's forgiveness will help you get on with your life in a fresh, new way.** Pause.

You should be standing in your original tight circle. Say: **As we close, let's pray silently for courage and wisdom in dealing with our sins as** ▶**people of character who admit their sins and accept God's forgiveness.** Allow a few moments of silent prayer, then close by saying "amen."

TEACHER

If you have limited class space, instruct people to take small steps backward and forward. You might also have people stand in two lines facing each other and have them step away from and toward each other.

◀ THE POINT

For Extra Time

NO COMPARISON
(up to 10 minutes)

Form groups of three or four. Have groups read 1 Samuel 13:1-15 and 15:1-31. Then direct group members to discuss the following questions:

- **Was it worse for Saul to disobey God or for David to commit adultery and murder? Explain.**

- **How was Saul's reaction to his sin like David's reaction to his sins? How was it different?**

- **How was God's response to Saul like God's response to David? How was it different?**

- **What does God's response to Saul teach about the results of not dealing with sin appropriately?**

AVOIDANCE TECHNIQUES
(up to 10 minutes)

Write each of the following words on an index card: "denial," "justification," "rationalization," "omission," and "lying." Divide the class into five groups, and give each group one of the cards. Have each group define its word as it relates to the avoidance of admitting sin and then create a 30-second role-play that illustrates the avoidance technique. For added fun, have the role-plays portray examples from people's childhoods in which they used these techniques.

After each group has presented its role-play, ask the entire class the following questions:

- **Which of these techniques do we seem to use most often?**

- **Why do you think we use these techniques more than others?**

- **Are some techniques worse than others? If so, which ones?**

- **How effective are these techniques with others? with God?**

- **Is God harder on us when we try to avoid admitting our sins? Explain.**

Dealing With  Sin

As a group, read aloud 2 Samuel 12:1-25. Then discuss the questions for your section of the handout. You have about seven minutes to complete your section of the handout.

Admitting Sin

- Why did Nathan tell David a story before he accused him directly?
- What do you think kept David from admitting his sins prior to this time?
- What are the important elements of David's confession of his sins?

Accepting Punishment

- In what specific ways did David resist God's punishment? accept it?
- To what extent was it acceptable for David to ask God to save his son?
- Why do you think David eventually accepted the death of his son?

Acknowledging Forgiveness

- How did God repair the damage of David's sins? What couldn't be repaired?
- What did David do to get on with life after he was punished for his sins?
- How did acknowledging God's forgiveness help David get on with his life?

SPILL THE BEANS

As a group, read the FYI box to the right and 2 Samuel 12:1-25. Then use what you've read to answer the following questions. You have 10 minutes to complete the handout.

HOW did David attempt to hide his sin from others? himself? God?

WHY do you think David took such drastic measures to hide his sin?

WHAT were the results of David's sin? of his attempt to hide his sin?

WHAT does this incident teach about our ability to hide our sins?

WHAT does this incident teach about how we should deal with our sins?

Admitting Sin

People of character admit their sins
and accept God's forgiveness.
2 Samuel 12:1-25

Reflecting on God's Word

Each day this week, read one of the following Scriptures, and examine what it teaches about confessing sin and accepting God's forgiveness. Then consider how you can respond to sin in a way that is acceptable to God. List your discoveries in the space under each passage.

Day 1: James 5:14-16. Sometimes unconfessed sin hinders our prayers.

Day 2: Romans 3:21-26. Everyone sins and thus needs God's forgiveness.

Day 3: Psalm 103:11-14. God removes our sins when we admit them.

Day 4: Leviticus 5:1-6. We should admit every sin that we are aware of.

Day 5: Romans 4:6-8. Forgiveness is one of God's greatest blessings.

Day 6: 1 John 1:8-10. Admitting our sins keeps us completely honest.

Beyond Reflection

Read James 5:16 and 1 John 1:9 each day for a week before your prayer time. Use these verses to remind you to make admitting your sins to God a daily prayer habit. That way sins don't pile up, become forgotten, or get discounted. Challenge yourself to use the words "admit," "sin," and "forgive" as part of every prayer during the week.

Coming Next Week: Honoring God (1 Samuel 13:14 and
2 Samuel 7:1-17)

Lesson 4

Honoring God

God honors people of character who seek to honor him.  ◀ **THE POINT**

OBJECTIVES

Participants will
- identify differences between God's honor and human honors,
- discover that God honors people who try to honor him, and
- learn how to honor God with obedient lives and acts of love.

BIBLE BASIS

Look up the Scriptures for this lesson. Then read the following background paragraphs to see how the passages relate to people today.

Shortly after Saul became king, he gave in to his fear of the people and disobeyed a direct order from God (1 Samuel 13:1-14). As a result of Saul's disobedience, God decided to end Saul's dynasty with Saul. Instead of appointing one of Saul's sons to Israel's throne, God was going to replace Saul with a leader "after his [God's] own heart." David was that leader.

1 SAMUEL 13:14

God didn't choose David because he was perfect—far from it. David, like Saul, was a perfectly fallible human who sometimes gave in to his sinful urges. However, David's life was characterized by obedience to God and a willingness to admit his occasional acts of disobedience. When God gave David a direct order, David followed it (1 Samuel 23:1-5; 30:7-10; 2 Samuel 2:1-2; 5:19-25). When God showed David his sins, David admitted them and asked God to forgive him (2 Samuel 12:13; 24:10-11).

God chose David to lead his people because David possessed the inner character that pleased God. David was a man after God's own heart who honored God on a daily basis through his obedience and his openness to admitting when he was wrong. Because David honored God in this way, God honored David by promising him that his dynasty would never end.

2 SAMUEL 7:1-17   As a man after God's own heart, David sought to honor God both with a life of obedience and with special acts of love. For example, 2 Samuel 7:1-17 describes how David tried to honor God by building him a temple. God declined David's offer but appreciated the heart behind the offer. Therefore, God honored David by promising to build him a dynasty that would never end.

In the ancient Near East, kings and emperors frequently built temples to honor their gods and to remind future generations of their—the kings'— greatness. Thus, it was customary for a king to chisel in the temple walls an inscription identifying himself as the builder and threatening with a terrible curse anyone who effaced or erased his name. In so doing, the king sought to maintain the memory of his dynasty forever.

Within this context, there was nothing noteworthy about David seeking to build a temple for Yahweh, the God of Israel. However, David's reasons for wanting to build a temple were highly unusual. First, David was troubled by the fact that he lived in a cedar palace while the ark of God was housed in a tent (2 Samuel 5:11; 6:17). The disparity in accommodations seemed to imply that David regarded himself as more important or more substantial than God. Yet nothing could have been further from the truth. Second, it appears that David wanted to build a house for God's "name" (see verse 13). Instead of chiseling his own name onto the temple, David probably wanted to inscribe God's name in stone so future generations would remember who was really king in Israel.

God so appreciated David's wish to honor him that he responded to David in kind. That is, God replaced David's plan to build God a "house" (= temple: verses 5, 6, 7, 13) with a promise to build David a "house" (= dynasty: verse 11). Unlike Saul's dynasty, which had died with Saul, David's dynasty would live forever. God would establish the kingdom of David's son (Solomon) and allow that son to build a temple in honor of his name. Moreover, when David's son sinned, God would discipline him but never desert him. Consequently, David's house and throne would last forever (in the person of Christ), and the memory of David would stand long after the temple he had hoped to build would have become a heap of stones.

Few, if any, of your class members can afford to construct a building in honor of God. However, all of them can honor God with their obedient lives and their own special acts of love. Use this lesson to help your class members discover that God val-

ues their attempts to honor him and that he will respond to
their efforts by returning honor to them.

THIS LESSON AT A GLANCE

Section	Minutes	What Participants Will Do	Supplies
OPENING	up to 10	**READ ALL ABOUT IT**—Compare reasons the world honors people with reasons God honors people.	Newspapers, highlighting pens
BIBLE EXPLORATION AND APPLICATION	30 to 40	☐ Option 1: **CHECK THIS OUT!**—Honor God with "offerings," discover how God responded to David's offer in 2 Samuel 7:1-17, and learn that God values their obedient lives and their special offerings.	Bibles, "Check This Out!" handout (p. 66), index cards, pencils, marker, newsprint, scissors, tape
	25 to 35	☐ Option 2: **HIGH HONORS**—Discuss what makes honor meaningful, then examine 1 Samuel 13:14 and 2 Samuel 7:1-17 to discover how and why God honors his people.	Bibles, "Divine Honors" handouts (p. 67), pencils
CLOSING	up to 10	**GOLD-STAR AWARDS**—Create gold-star bookmarks as a reminder to honor God because God will return that honor.	Index cards, gold foil stars, scissors
FOR EXTRA TIME	up to 10	**WISDOM AND HONOR**—Examine various proverbs to discover what inner characteristics receive honor.	Bibles
	up to 10	**COURSE REFLECTION**—Evaluate the course and suggest ways it might be improved.	

Read All About It

(up to 10 minutes)

Before class, collect the sports, business, entertainment, and obituaries sections from several newspapers. Collect one section for every two class members.

Form groups of four. Give each group two newspaper sections and a highlighting pen. Say: **Working as a group, glance through your newspaper sections and highlight every report of someone being honored, praised, or given an award. After five minutes, we'll discuss what you find.**

When time is up, ask the entire class these questions:

● **Who was being honored in the articles? How were they being honored?**

● **Were they being honored more for their character or for their achievements?**

● **To what extent do you think God honors these people as the world does?**

● **How is God's honor like the world's honor? How is it different?**

Say: **For the past few weeks, we've been examining different aspects of David's inner character. We've discovered that God valued David for who he was and not just for what he could do. Today we're going to conclude our study of David's character by discussing how David sought to honor God and how God responded. We'll discover that** ▶**God honors people of character who seek to honor him.**

THE POINT ▷

☐ **OPTION 1:**

Check This Out!

(30 to 40 minutes)

Before class, make one copy of the "Check This Out!" handout (p. 66) for every two people. Cut apart the checks. Write the following amounts on separate index cards: $10; $1,000; $100,000. Create one index card for every four people, repeating the different dollar amounts as necessary.

Keep people in their groups of four. Give each group four checks, one of the index cards, and a pencil. Say: **One way we** honor God is by supporting his work with our money. In your group, decide how you want to use the money you've been allocated to honor God. For example, you might contribute to a church building program, a Bible society, a missionary, or a local charity. When you decide how you want to spend your money, fill out your checks accordingly.

After several minutes, ask groups to report how they allocated their funds. Then instruct group members to discuss the following questions. After each question, ask for volunteers to report their groups' responses. Ask:

● How did you feel as you were deciding how to allocate your money? when you heard the other groups report what they had given?

● Did some groups honor God more than yours? If so, how was their honor better?

● How does the amount of money given affect the way we view the amount of honor given?

● How is this activity like the ways we honor God in real life? How is it different?

Say: **It's easy to feel that the people who honor God most are those with lots of money or incredible talents—people like David. But 2 Samuel 7:1-17 tells us that God honored David for reasons unrelated to his wealth and his abilities.**

Instruct group members to read **2 Samuel 7:1-17.** While people are reading, write the following questions on a sheet of newsprint, and hang it where everyone can see it:
● Why did David want to construct a house for God?
● How do you think God felt about David's proposal?
● Why do you think God turned down David's offer?
● How did God bless David for trying to honor him?

When groups finish reading, have them spend approximately eight minutes discussing the questions.

When time is up, ask for volunteers to summarize their groups' insights for the rest of the class. Then have group members answer the following questions:

● **What is most important in honoring God? What is least important?**

● **How does God feel when we try to honor him? How does God respond?**

Say: **David was far more than a wealthy king with the financial resources to build a temple in honor of God. According to 1 Samuel 13:14, he was also a man after God's own heart whose life was characterized by obedience to God.** Ask:

● **How was David's inner character revealed in his**

wish to build a temple? demonstrated in his daily obedience?

● **How should we honor God through the use of our money? in our daily lives?**

Say: **It's often easy to honor God simply by writing out a check. However, God values our daily obedience as much as he appreciates our weekly offerings. Both ways of honoring God are valid and acceptable when they arise out of a godly character.**

Give a blank check from the "Check This Out!" handout to each person and a pencil to anyone who needs one. Say: **David honored God with his financial resources and with his obedient life. Think for a moment about how God might want you to honor him this week. Then write your idea on your check in the space where you would normally write the amount of money. When everyone in your group finishes writing, tell your group members what you'll do to honor God.**

Allow several minutes for people to write and report, then say: ▶**God honors people of character who seek to honor him. Therefore, we should honor God with an obedient life and with our own acts of love. As we do, we'll discover that the only joy greater than giving honor to God is receiving honor from God.**

T H E   P O I N T ▷

■■■■■■■■■■■■■■■■■■■■■■■■

For *Even Deeper* Discussion

Form groups of four to discuss the following questions.

● How do you think God feels about illegal attempts to honor him, such as smuggling Bibles, blowing up abortion clinics, or sharing the gospel when it's against the law? To what extent does God honor people for being sincere? for doing the right thing? for both?

● Do you think God looks more at our actions or our motives when he decides how to honor us? Explain. To what extent can good motives justify misguided actions? To what extent do bad motives discredit good actions?

■■■■■■■■■■■■■■■■■■■■■■■■

☐   **O P T I O N   2 :**

High Honors

(25 to 35 minutes)

Before class, make one photocopy of the "Divine Honors" handout (p. 67) for each person.

Say: **Undoubtedly every one of you has been praised or honored for something you've done. Maybe you were patted on the back by a favorite teacher or a supervisor at work. Perhaps you were given a special award for some outstanding achievement. Whatever the case, being praised or honored probably made a strong impression on you.**

Instruct people to form pairs. Have partners each describe some meaningful praise, honor, or award they have received. After several minutes, have partners each tell about some praise, honor, or award they have received that didn't mean much to them.

After several minutes, have each pair join another pair to form a group of four. Have group members discuss the following questions. After each question, ask for volunteers to report their groups' responses. Ask:

- **How did you feel when you received the meaningful honor? the insignificant honor?**

- **What made one honor meaningful to you? Why was the other honor insignificant?**

- **What do your experiences reveal about the essential elements of meaningful honor?**

Say: **Everyone likes to receive honor, especially when it's from the right person and for the right reasons. Of course, the best honor we can receive is the honor that God gives us. So let's examine how and why God honored David as a person of character.**

Give each person a copy of the "Divine Honors" handout and a pencil. Instruct groups to follow the instructions at the top of the handout.

After eight minutes, ask groups to report their insights. Then ask the entire class the following questions:

- **For what reasons does God honor people?**

- **In what ways does God honor people?**

- **How should we respond when God honors us?**

Say: **God honored David by making David king and by promising to maintain David's royal line forever. ▶God honors people of character who seek to honor him, so we should thank God for honoring us in the past and develop the character traits that God will want to honor in the future.**

Instruct people to write their answers to the questions at the bottom of the "Divine Honors" handout. After several minutes, have group members share what they wrote.

Say: **Psalm 112 lists a number of benefits that come to people of good inner character. Verse 9 promises**

TEACHER
TIP

For variety, consider having people sit across from each other in two equal rows two to three feet apart. Have people each describe the meaningful praise with the person across from them and then move one seat to the right and discuss the insignificant honor with their new partners. You can continue to have people discuss and move one seat to the right with the questions that follow or with the Bible study questions on the "Divine Honors" handout.

BIBLE
INSIGHT

According to 1 Samuel 13:14, God rejected Saul for disobedience and then began the process of replacing Saul by seeking "for himself a man after his own heart." David was the person in view, for later on God sent Samuel to anoint David with the explanation, "I have seen for myself a king" (1 Samuel 16:1). David was an obedient person after God's own heart, so God chose him to replace Saul.

◀ THE POINT

that the righteous will be exalted in honor. Just as we saw in the life of David, ▷God honors people of character who seek to honor him. During the coming week, read Psalm 112 once a day to remind you of the ways God has honored you and to help you develop the character that God will honor.

■ ■

FOR *Even Deeper* DISCUSSION

Form groups of four to discuss the following questions.

● Read Genesis 12:3 and 1 Samuel 2:30. How is being honored by God like being blessed by God? How is it different? To what extent does God honor people based on what they do? based on God's grace?

● How can we influence God's decision to honor us? To what extent is it proper to seek God's honor on our lives? What are appropriate ways of seeking God's honor? When might seeking God's honor become inappropriate or wrong?

■ ■

Apply·It·To·Life™
This Week!

The "Apply-It-To-Life This Week!" handout (p. 68) helps people further explore the issues uncovered in today's class. Give everyone a photocopy of the handout. Encourage class members to take time during the coming week to explore the questions and activities on the handout.

CLOSING

Gold-Star Awards

(up to 10 minutes)

Before class, cut enough index cards into 1×5-inch strips so each class member will have one strip. Hand each person three gold foil stars and a card strip. Then instruct people to form pairs.

Say: **When we examine the whole of David's life, we see that David's desire to honor God with a temple was not an unusual act. It was simply one expression of David's lifelong commitment to honor and obey. Just as God honored David for seeking to honor him, God honors us as we seek to honor him.** Pause.

Briefly tell your partner one way you think God has honored you in the past. Then stick a star on your card strip. Allow two minutes for partners to share. Then say:

Now tell your partner one way you feel God honoring your life today. When you're done, stick another star on the card strip. Allow two minutes for people to talk, then say: **Finally, tell your partner one honorable character trait you'd like to nurture this week. Then stick the last star on your card strip.**

When everyone finishes, say: **Keep this gold-star award in your Bible as a bookmark to remind you to honor God every day because ▶ God honors people of character who seek to honor him.** Close in prayer, asking God to help people develop the character that honors him and thanking God for the example of David's life.

◀ **THE POINT**

 For Extra Time

WISDOM AND HONOR
(up to 10 minutes)

Form groups of four. Assign each group two of the following verses from Proverbs: 3:35; 13:18; 15:33; 20:3; 21:21; 22:4; 26:1; and 29:23. Instruct groups to read their verses and then discuss what they teach about the character traits that lead to honor.

Allow five minutes for discussion, then ask the entire class the following questions:

- **What inner characteristics lead to a person receiving honor?**

- **How are these inner characteristics shown in outer actions?**

- **How will these characteristics be honored by God? by people?**

COURSE REFLECTION
(up to 10 minutes)

Ask class members to reflect on the four lessons on David. Then have them take turns completing the following sentences:

- **Something I learned in this course was...**

- **If I told friends about this course, I'd say...**

- **Something I'll do differently because of this course is...**

Then ask people what they liked most about the course and how they might change the course. Please note their comments (along with your own), and send them to the Adult Curriculum Editor at Group Publishing, Inc., Box 481, Loveland, CO, 80539. We want your feedback so we can make each course we publish better than the one before it. Thanks!

Check This Out!

630-9847898-134258-43

001

Pay to the
Order of: _____ $ [   ]

_____ Dollars

First Trust Bank

Signed _____

630-9847898-134258-43

002

Pay to the
Order of: _____ $ [   ]

_____ Dollars

First Trust Bank

Signed _____

630-9847898-134258-43

003

Pay to the
Order of: _____ $ [   ]

_____ Dollars

First Trust Bank

Signed _____

630-9847898-134258-43

004

Pay to the
Order of: _____ $ [   ]

_____ Dollars

First Trust Bank

Signed _____

Divine Honors

As a group, read
1 Samuel 13:14, the information
in the FYI box, and 2 Samuel 7:1-17.
Then answer the first four questions below. After
eight minutes you'll report your insights to the rest of
the class.

FOR YOUR INFORMATION

According to 1 Samuel 13:14, God rejected Saul for disobedience and then began the process of replacing Saul by seeking "for himself a man after his own heart." David was the person in view, for later on God sent Samuel to anoint David with the explanation, "I have seen for myself a king" (1 Samuel 16:1). David was an obedient person after God's own heart, so God chose him to replace Saul.

● ●

● How did God honor David's inner character of obedience?

● How did God honor David's wish to construct a temple?

● To what extent did God honor David for what David did?

● To what extent did God honor David for who David was?

● ●

● What is one way God has honored you in the past? Why do you think God honored you in this way?

● What's one inner character trait you want to develop and have God honor you for in the future?

Apply·It·To·Life™ This Week!

Honoring God

God honors people of character who seek to honor him.
1 Samuel 13:14 and 2 Samuel 7:1-17

Reflecting on God's Word

Each day this week, read one of the following Scriptures, and examine what it teaches about honoring God and responding to God's honor in our lives. Then consider how you can honor God in new ways every day. List your insights in the space under each passage.

Day 1: Psalm 91:14-16. God honors and upholds us during times of distress.

Day 2: 1 Peter 2:16-17. We honor God by giving other people the proper honor.

Day 3: Proverbs 3:9-10. God honors people who honor him with their income.

Day 4: Luke 14:7-11. We should wait for God to honor us at the right time.

Day 5: 1 Samuel 2:30. God promises to honor people who seek to honor him.

Day 6: Hebrews 13:18. We can enjoy clear consciences when we act honorably.

Beyond Reflection

Seek new ways to honor God and to identify ways God honors you in return. Draw a line down the center of a sheet of paper to create two columns. Write "I will honor God" at the top of one column and "God honored me" at the top of the other. Then begin each day by thinking of one way you want to honor God that day. For example, you might contribute your time to a charity, write a caring note to a friend, or tell someone about God's love. Write your idea in the "I will honor God" column. At the end of the day, put a check mark beside your idea if you did it. Then write one way God honored you during the day in the "God honored me" column. Periodically review your "honor roll" as a reminder of the importance of honoring God and being honored by God.

Fellowship and Outreach Specials

Use the following activities any time you want. You can use them as part of (or in place of) your regular class activities, or you might consider planning a special event based on one or more of the ideas.

A View to David

Gather your class for a movie night at which you view Group's Ancient Secrets of the Bible video titled *Battle of David and Goliath: Truth or Myth?* This video re-enacts the battle between David and the 9-foot Philistine giant who foolishly mocked the army of God. After viewing the video, serve refreshments and ask the following questions that tie this story to the lessons in this course.

- **Was David's desire to defeat Goliath a sinful urge? Why or why not? To what extent are desires for vengeance justified if the action is to avenge God? his people?**
- **How did Goliath's defeat bring peace to the people of Israel? In what ways was David's battle with Goliath an example of biblical peacemaking?**
- **What aspects of David's inner character were revealed in his encounter with the Philistine gargantuan? How did David's actions strengthen his faith? other people's faith?**

Inside Out

Volunteer as a group at a local service organization that feeds, clothes, shelters, or otherwise provides for people in need. Your presence and willingness to help will be wonderful outer examples of the inner character God desires his people to nurture. While you serve the people in need, affirm them for the commendable aspects of their inner character, and remind them that God values their inner character even when their outer circumstances are difficult.

An Ounce of Prevention!

One of the best ways to promote peace is to practice kindness. Have class members create Care Cards to distribute to members of your church or to people in their families and neighborhoods. Provide index cards, colorful markers, and a variety of rubber stamps and colorful ink pads to decorate the cards. Have adults add affirming messages such as "Your smile and kind ways make a difference!" or "Thanks for being who you are!" Challenge each class member to create three cards and to distribute them before next week's class.

Heart for Peace

When David asked Nabal to break out the food to feed his army, a war nearly broke out instead! Celebrate David's change of heart and Abigail's skillful peacemaking with a Heart-for-Peace soup night. Have the class prepare a simple, buffet-style meal for your entire church to enjoy. Include several soups or chili and crusty, warm bread. Ask several class members to make photocopies of affirming Scriptures such as Matthew 5:9; Hebrews 12:14a; and James 3:18. Place a basket of the verses at the end of the buffet line and encourage everyone to take a slip of paper to read and to keep as a reminder of the importance of peacemaking.

Delving Deeper

Invite class members to form a study group to examine other events from David's life. For example, people might study David's friendship with Jonathan (1 Samuel 19:1-7; 20:1-42), his sparing of Saul's life (24:1-22; 26:1-25), his mourning for Saul and Jonathan (2 Samuel 1:1-27), his bringing of the ark of God to Jerusalem (6:1-23), or his census of the people (24:1-25; 1 Chronicles 21:1–22:1). Focus each study session on discovering aspects of David's inner character that God wants people to imitate or to avoid.

Apply-It-To-Life™ Together

Create a meeting based on the "Apply-It-To-Life This Week!" handouts from the course. As a part of the meeting, ask volunteers to share what they discovered through each of the handouts. During the meeting, have people choose at least two "Beyond Reflection" activities to complete together. Establish a schedule with goals for the completion of each of the activities they select.

David: Developing Personal Character

Please help Group Publishing, Inc., continue to provide innovative and useful resources for adult ministry by taking a moment to fill out and send us this evaluation. Thanks!

Did you read the Introduction (pp. 5-12)?

❏ YES ❏ NO

If so, what was most helpful about it? least helpful?

Did you use the art on the Publicity Page (p. 13)?

❏ YES ❏ NO

If so, what about it did you like most? least?

Please mark which of the following activities you used:

	LESSON 1	LESSON 2	LESSON 3	LESSON 4
Opening	❏	❏	❏	❏
BE & A Option 1	❏	❏	❏	❏
BE & A Option 2	❏	❏	❏	❏
Closing	❏	❏	❏	❏
For Extra Time 1	❏	❏	❏	❏
For Extra Time 2	❏	❏	❏	❏

Circle the words that best describe the following aspects of the course. Feel free to add suggestions for improvement below each question.

How helpful was the information in the Bible Basis sections?

poor   fair   average   good   excellent

How effectively did the lessons help people discover biblical truths?

poor   fair   average   good   excellent

How well did the lessons help people apply biblical truths to their lives?

poor   fair   average   good   excellent

How many of the four "Apply-It-To-Life This Week!" handouts did you distribute?

none   one   two   three   four

Which of the Fellowship and Outreach Specials did you use?

What did you like most about *David: Developing Personal Character?*

What would you change about *David: Developing Personal Character?*

Get Any Size Adult Group Exploring...
Discussing...Learning...and *Applying* God's Word!

Here's everything you need to lead *any* size class—in *one* money-saving book!
- •Complete 4-session courses!
- •No extra student books needed!
- •No waste—photocopiable handouts!
- •Sure-fire discussion-starters included!

With **Apply-It-To-Life™ Adult Bible Curriculum**, you'll teach like Jesus taught—with *active learning*! Your adult learners will participate in activities and then share with others in the group. Together you'll grow in friendship...fellowship...and living out the Gospel.

Teach with confidence! Every lesson includes a thorough explanation of the Scripture text—you'll be prepared!

Teach new and mature Christians at the same time! You'll lead purposeful, nonthreatening discussions that let everyone participate...and learn!

TITLES INCLUDE:

Title	ISBN
The Bible: What's in It for Me?	1-55945-504-7
The Church: What Am I Doing Here?	1-55945-513-6
Communication: Enhancing Your Relationships	1-55945-512-8
David: Developing Personal Character	1-55945-506-3
Discovering God's Will for Your Life	1-55945-507-1
Evangelism for Every Day	1-55945-515-2
Faith in the Workplace	1-55945-514-4
Finding Relevance in Old Testament	1-55945-523-3
Freedom: Seeing Yourself As God Sees You	1-55945-502-0
Genesis: Understanding God's Goodness	1-55945-517-9
High-Impact Christianity	1-55945-503-9
Honest to God: Prayer for Every Day	1-55945-518-7
Jesus	1-55945-500-4
Strengthening Family Relationships	1-55945-501-2
Too Busy? A Biblical Approach to Life Management	1-55945-516-0

Order today from your local Christian bookstore, or write: Group Publishing, Box 485, Loveland, CO 80539.